T0120715

There's Always Hope No Matter What

a companion booklet for caregivers to the
No Matter What Devotional for Youth

TOMMYE WILLIAMS

WESTBOW
PRESS®
A DIVISION OF THOMAS NELSON
& ZONDERVAN

WestBow Press books may be ordered through booksellers or by contacting:

WestBow Press
A Division of Thomas Nelson & Zondervan
1663 Liberty Drive
Bloomington, IN 47403
www.westbowpress.com
844-714-3454

Scripture quotations are taken from the New King James Version. Copyright © 1982 by Thomas Nelson, Inc. Used by permission. All rights reserved.

ISBN: 978-1-6642-9268-0 (sc)
ISBN: 978-1-6642-9269-7 (e)

Library of Congress Control Number: 2023903551

Print information available on the last page.

WestBow Press rev. date: 03/15/2023

CONTENTS

In memory of my beloved grandmother,
Mrs. Tommye J. Moore

ACKNOWLEDGMENTS

I have dedicated this book and its companion devotional *No Matter What There's Always Hope* to the memory of my grandmother, the late Mrs. Tommye J. Moore. She was a great blessing in my life. She loved God all her life and always had hope no matter what adverse circumstances she faced in childhood and adulthood. Although her family was poor and she grew up without a father, she was rich in faith, and God was the anchor of her life. She became a widow at a young age with four children ages eight months to thirteen years to raise. Later she became a caregiver to her brother, affectionately known as "Uncle Brother," who was a disabled US Army veteran. My grandmother always had hope no matter what came her way. She prospered in life and was a tremendous blessing not only to her family but to countless others.

I would also like to express my gratitude to my sister, Yvette, for her unwavering support throughout this project, starting when it was just an expressed interest I voiced, and for the feedback and insight she provided. A big thank-you goes to Gabby for the administrative support she provided in the midst of her super busy schedule. I also would like to thank my co-laborer in the children's church ministry, Ciji, who regularly sent me reminders and words of encouragement about getting these books out of my head and onto paper.

And most of all, I am truly honored and grateful to my Heavenly Father for entrusting me with this assignment and for His leadership in bringing it to fruition.

PREFACE

The Lord has entrusted me with a message of hope for troubled youth and for caregivers, and I must be obedient to share what God has revealed to me. My urgent and compelling motivation for writing this caregivers' booklet is pleasing God and helping troubled youth overcome adversity. I hope to expose, push back, and shine the light on the darkness of hopelessness that is impacting this generation, and to bring forth truth, insight, and revelation about the power of hope and the influence caregivers have in transforming lives.

Childhood trauma is one of the greatest attackers of hope that one will ever face. Childhood trauma—affliction and adversity in childhood—can come in many forms, such as abandonment, fatherlessness, rejection, generational trauma, low self-worth, low self-esteem, and abuse. But the good news is that things that caused pain, hurt, and affliction in our young people's past do not have to control their future. God is in the business of rebuilding and restoring lives. He restores broken lives with hope.

Many a time have they afflicted me from
my youth:
Yet they have not prevailed against me.
(Psalm 129:2)

INTRODUCTION

Young people have always held a special place in my heart. Ever since I was a child, I envisioned that part of my future would be to serve as a mother figure and cheerleader to a houseful of kids—kids who were not my biological offspring, kids who had been abused, abandoned, overlooked, rejected, or neglected. That vision has stayed with me all my life, and I believe it to have been prophetic.

Part of fulfilling that vision has been writing the devotional for youth titled *No Matter What There's Always Hope*, the companion devotional to the book you are holding in your hands. Although no children or youth at present are physically under my roof, I wrote the youth devotional *No Matter What There's Always Hope* with the heart of a mother and a cheerleader. I am on an assignment from God to instill or restore hope in the hearts and minds of each and every person, young or old, who reads that devotional. My heart especially goes out to youth who are troubled or feel hopeless, or who have been traumatized as a result of adverse childhood experiences. I believe that hope is a key to helping them break free from the chains of the past. I believe that hope will ultimately lead them to a confident expectation that better days are ahead.

The Bible says "hope deferred makes the heart sick: but when the desire comes it is a tree of life" (Proverbs 13:12). I believe that now is the time for the tree of life (hope) to spring forth in our young people's lives and for their hearts to be healed from past hurts and wounds—for hope to no longer be delayed, and that their faith and hope be in God. (1 Peter 1:21)

And I believe that you, as a caregiver, can make a difference in young people's lives, and that you can be used as an instrument by God to foster hope in the youth who are assigned to your care. You can be a hope carrier, encouraging young people by stirring up hope in their lives. It is my prayer that as you read this book, you will be encouraged, strengthened, reaffirmed, and gain insight, wisdom, and strategy about what you can do to help restore hope to the youth you have been assigned to. I believe that it's by God's design that you are reading this book, and that it will become your go-to toolkit for strategies for impacting lives through the power of hope. If you are a caregiver in any capacity, whether you are a parent, grandparent, aunt or uncle, godparent, foster parent, case worker, teacher, coach, probation officer, counselor, or have authority or influence in a young person's life, and you desire to be a part of the process for restoring hope to youth in your sphere of influence, this book is for you.

I believe that this book will also provide refreshment, nourishment, and encouragement for your soul, and that your own hope will be renewed, as I know that your job or role as a caregiver is not an easy one. And I pray that as you sow into the youth assigned to you, you will reap a blessing.

> He who refreshes others will also be refreshed. (Proverbs 11:25b NIV)

I pray that you will receive a fresh revelation about the impact of your influence and that you will be a hope carrier to those young people who are in your sphere of influence. I pray that you will be motivated and determined to help youth overcome pessimistic mindsets about the future by encouraging them to establish goals and find pathways to achieve those goals. And as you encourage the youth and cheer them on as they establish and achieve short term goals, they will gain confidence to establish and achieve long term goals (aspirations) for the future. They will have hope.

I also pray that "your hearts will be flooded with light so that you can understand the confident hope He has given to those He called." (Ephesians 1:18 NLT) because understanding the hope for which you, as a caregiver, have been called, is so important. I salute you and am cheering for you because I believe that yours is a noble calling that often goes unnoticed. But

God sees you and He will reward you. Your efforts are not in vain.

I also pray that you will be encouraged and that your strength will be renewed as you read this book. I pray with confident expectation (hope) because I know that this is God's will and when we ask anything according to His will, He hears us.

This book (toolkit) combines practical concepts based on research with spiritual truths and provides strategies that caregivers can use to build or restore hope in children and youth who are suffering from what I call "The Terrible Ds" (more about that in chapter 2). This two-pronged approach, combining the practical with the spiritual, is God's blueprint for victory. The practical approach, the science of hope, offers strategies or pathways to restoring hope in youth for a brighter future; however, the spiritual approach plays an even greater role in restoring hope. It is vitally important for children and youth to believe in a loving God, for them to know the depths of God's love for them, for them to learn about and believe in the truth of God's Word, and for them to have a cheerleader in their lives to support and encourage them. Scientific research on trauma survivors validates this belief.

Scientific research is clear that spiritual faith and spiritual support are key to raising one's hope from low hope (hopelessness) to high hope (confidence in the future). And as hope carriers, we need to make room for children and youth to access a loving God.

The companion youth devotional gives youth space to express themselves, to unlock their emotions, and it introduces them to their Heavenly Father. That devotional is a way for youth to learn how to access a loving God. And when children and youth know the depths of God's love for them, it will ultimately lead them to casting away fears or feelings of hopelessness about their future.

CHAPTER 1

God Had a Plan

In October 2020, I was one of four women asked to speak at the meeting of our women's ministry on its third anniversary. We were asked to speak on the topic of being a servant. Before the meeting, each of us was given individualized questions that the members of the ministry wanted us to address. As I was searching the scriptures in response to one of the questions, I stumbled across Romans 12:11, which says in part "be fervent in spirit serving the Lord." And that was a wonderful answer for that question. But I kept on reading, and the verse that followed, Romans 12:12, jumped out at me and resonated in my spirit: "be joyful in hope, patient in tribulation, and consistent in prayer." God illuminated that verse, specifically "be joyful in hope," and I knew that it was a revelation from Him and that flesh and blood did not reveal that to me.

I believe God chose me to carry the message of hope because I have always held on to hope, no matter what it looked like. I've sat in a courtroom where my son was falsely charged with a serious crime and the prosecutor, police, and probation officer joined forces against him, but I held on to hope and stood on God's Word, and God was faithful to come through; charges against my son were ultimately dismissed "in the interest of justice." I had instances of unjust actions taken against me at work by a newly hired executive officer who wanted to make a name for himself; the plan was to use me as a scapegoat for something that I had nothing to do with that had caused him embarrassment. I stated my objection to this injustice orally, but it fell on deaf ears, and again in writing, also typing up some scriptures that addressed my situation. I let it go but held on to hope and stood on God's Word. And God came through. As a matter of fact, the newly hired executive who came against me was subsequently fired, and his firing made front-page headlines in the *LA Times.*

I have countless other stories of hope and standing on God's Word with the expectation that He would come through, and God has been faithful. Hope is what has kept me during the difficult seasons. Hope is my anchor.

Although I likely had read Romans 12:12 numerous times before that meeting, when I read it on that occasion, it leaped into my spirit. *Wow!* I said to myself. *This verse holds the key to overcoming life's challenges.* And when I read the first part of the verse, "be joyful in hope," I knew I had to do something with what God had revealed to me. And so I dubbed it The Hope Project.

The Journey Begins

I started this God-inspired Hope Project by sharing Romans 12:12 with others. I also started jotting down scriptures dealing with hope as I ran across them. I knew that God wanted me to do something with the topic. Then in 2021, I began to focus my attention on hope as it relates to children and youth, especially as it pertains to young people who have experienced hopelessness as a result of childhood trauma.

In 2021, my sister told me about a training program for LA County Juvenile Probation Department staff on the topic of the science of hope as it relates to children and youth. I had the opportunity to listen in on the training, and this was another *wow* moment for me. The presenters, Casey Gwinn, JD, and Chan Hellman, PhD, spoke about the science of hope and how it can change lives, including lives of troubled youth, when put into practice. When I heard their presentation, I knew that this was a godsend. I did more research on the topic and was convinced that combining the science of hope theory (practical) with the spiritual is a blueprint for victory.

In a nutshell, scientific research has proven that hope can be measured (science of hope) and that hope is a learned way of thinking about oneself in relation to goals—not only in formulating goals (willpower) but in taking the necessary steps to achieve those goals ("waypower"). Hope is what links someone who has a troubled past to an expectation that better days are ahead. The theory behind the science of hope is that hope is the sum of the mental willpower and waypower that one has for their goals—as the saying goes, "where there's a will, there's a way". The science of hope strategies are embodied in the companion youth devotional.

In July 2022, I received a generic email about a writer's challenge workshop. Since I knew I would eventually share the message of hope through written form, I paid the $20 registration fee and signed up, as I sensed that this workshop was another godsend. The three-day workshop ran July 25–29. The sessions were only forty-five minutes long but powerful. God spoke to me during this workshop, and I knew I had a God-directed mandate to immediately start writing. This history of events culminated in the publishing and release of 2 books: the youth devotional and its companion book for caregivers. God had a plan.

CHAPTER 2

The Terrible Ds

Hopelessness is one of the most destructive mindsets that can rear its ugly head in the thoughts and minds of youth who may be assigned to our care. Before we can help to build or restore hope in them, we must first understand the root cause of lost hope or hopelessness. Hopelessness, or what science of hope proponents call "low hope," is often manifested in what I call "the Terrible Ds."

The Terrible Ds are feelings that can cause a person to think of themselves as hopeless. These feelings can include disheartenment, disappointment, discouragement, disillusionment, dismay, distress, despair, depression, defeat, desolation, despondency, and disconnection. Sadly, there is a strong possibility that a youth in your care has experienced or is currently experiencing one or more of these Terrible Ds.

Most, if not all, of the Terrible Ds have their root in rejection. In his book *Break Every Chain*, John Eckhardt describes rejection as a sense of being unwanted; the pain of desperately wanting people to love you while being convinced that they do not; to have an aching desire to be a part of something but never to feel that you are. Eckhardt goes on to say that rejection often starts at a young age—and can even start in the womb. There can be prenatal rejection, family rejection, or societal rejection. To compensate for rejection, some youth become isolated or withdrawn, like a turtle retreating into its shell for protection; others explode with anger, hatred, or rebellion. So rejection is a powerful tool used by the enemy to rob children of hope.

There may also be genetic or generational tendencies and dispositions that impact young people's lives. Research has confirmed that trauma can be passed down through generations. According to an article in *Scientific American*, "adverse experiences can change epigenetic pathways."[1]

I would add hard-heartedness, stiff-heartedness, impudence, and insolence to Eckhardt's list of things youth may do to compensate for rejection because as caregivers we often see these traits or behaviors in youth assigned to us. But we must see beneath the surface to understand the root cause of their behavior and to not give up hope on them. We must pray that their hearts will be softened as they come

---

[1] Rachel Yehuda, "How Parents' Trauma Leaves Biological Traces in Children," Scientific American (July 1, 2022), accessed January 16, 2023, https://www.scientificamerican.com/article/how-parents-rsquo-trauma-leaves-biological-traces-in-children.

to understand and believe that they are valuable, that they matter, that God loves them, and that He has a plan and purpose for their lives.

> "The thief comes only to kill, steal and destroy; I have come that they may have life and have it to the full." (John 10:10 NIV)

CHAPTER 3

What Is Hope?

Biblical hope is forward-looking faith. It is a confident belief based not on things experienced but on the Word of God. It is a joyful expectation for a good outcome. It is an optimistic assurance that something will be fulfilled.

Scientific hope is the sum of the mental willpower and waypower that a person has for their goals. Willpower is the driving force in hopeful thinking, while waypower is the mental plan or roadmap to guide hopeful thoughts. Willpower and waypower are processes involving what we think about ourselves in relation to our goals. From a spiritual perspective, willpower and waypower are based on a young person's sense of value and self-worth because they know they are loved, that their life matters, and that they are valuable to God. This sense of self-worth can give youth an optimistic mindset in terms of achieving goals. And achievement of goals leads to hope for the future.

Why Hope?

Hope is so important because it is the foundation on which we live and build our lives. It is what links our present and our past to the future. The Bible says, "let hope be the anchor for your soul" (Hebrews 6:19). Hope is like an anchor that can hold us in life's fiercest storms. Hope gives you a confident expectation for the future, no matter what current circumstances look like. Hope is about looking forward to the future. Hope involves your perception that goals can be met. When you are anchored to hope, you have the best chance to overcome challenges and navigate difficulties in life. Hope gives you the ability to look at any situation and know that regardless of how it may appear, God is going to come through.

Hope can make a tough situation more bearable.

Hope saves lives and changes lives.

Hope is a catalyst for breakthroughs and for dreams to come to pass.

Hope is believing in the omnipotence of God.

Your Role in Restoring Hope

Reading the foreword to the book *Cheering for Our Children,* by Casey Gwinn, brought tears to my eyes when I read, "All children need at least one person to passionately love, cheer for, affirm, encourage, and believe in them." Gwinn ends that paragraph by adding, "But there are millions of children growing up in this country every year who are profoundly impacted by childhood trauma and don't have anyone cheering for them." Those words are heart-wrenching.

But God has a plan—a plan to restore or renew hope in those youth who are experiencing the Terrible Ds. And I believe that God's plan for restored hope includes you. I believe God wants you to be a hope carrier and help change the way youth assigned to you think about their future. But I want you to know that God will do the heavy lifting in the process of restoring hope. You can help by implementing strategies found in the following section titled Pathway to Hope and then leave the results to God.

As you help in restoring hope in the youth assigned to your care, I want to reiterate that your efforts are not in vain. It has been proven that restoring hope in youth leads to significant improvement in school and emotional, physical, mental and social well-being. A high-hope mindset will have a positive impact on their ability to dream and have aspirations for the future.

CHAPTER 4

Pathway to Hope

It bears repeating that trauma and adversity can rob youth of hope, and loss of hope is a process that takes place over time. However, we can help youth push back against apathy and hopelessness by giving them spiritual and practical tools that will provide them with a pathway to hope. Caregivers can be carriers of hope to the youth in their sphere of influence through showing empathy, encouragement, and support. Children and youth need to know that their life has value, that their life has worth, that their life matters, that they are significant, and that they are capable of establishing and achieving goals. They need to know that they have a future and can look up and look forward to better days ahead, no matter what their current circumstances are. They need to learn how to silence the inner critic that tells them, *"you can't do it"*. They need to see themselves as God sees them. That's God's plan.

So let's take a look at strategies you can employ to help youth on their pathway to hope.

- See yourself as an instrument of change.
- Be a hope-giver.
- Speak life. Words are powerful.
- Instill hope by matching hope to a concrete goal.
- Be a cheerleader. Cheer them on.
- Look beyond and see beneath their attitude or action to determine what is driving it, and then prayerfully address it and renounce it.
- Allow youth to lament but not to stay stuck in their sorrow. Assure them that things will get better. "Weeping may endure for a night, but joy comes in the morning."
- Help youth change the way they feel about their future by having them talk and think about a vision for their life.
- Help them write down their vision.
- Affirm them. Remind them of their value and worth.
- See them the way God sees them. There are seeds of greatness in them.
- Help them deconstruct their negative thinking and to reconstruct it with hope-filled thinking that is based on the Word of God.
- Help them identify their strengths.
- Focus on their strengths and point them to the future.

- Help them identify their dreams and keep their dreams alive.
- Help them establish short-term goals they can aim for that are achievable. Create an ongoing process for achieving their goal with a fun activity.
- Show them, or help them identify, steps to achieve their short-term goals.
- Celebrate the small wins.
- Have caring conversations and listen actively so that they know that they matter.
- Remind them and continually reiterate that they are uniquely designed by God—that there is no one else on the earth exactly like them.
- Point them to Jesus, who is the essence of hope.
- Remind them that God has a special plan for their lives.
- Remind them that they have an incredible future ahead of them.
- Remind them that they have a loving Heavenly Father who will never leave them nor forsake them, that He is all-powerful, and that His perfect love will cast away all fears.
- Remind them that God's Word is truth.
- Remind them that their life matters.

The Hope Hierarchy: My Theory

In an effort to bring clarity to the somewhat abstract concept of how hope evolves (Hope Hierarchy) I have delineated the process that I believe leads one to hope. This theory is based on my belief that hope starts with having a relationship with God and knowing that God loves you, then building upon that foundational truth. There are five steps in the hierarchy of hope. You can use this hope hierarchy list as a tool to remind you about the steps involved in instilling or restoring hope in youth who feel hopeless. You can also use it to gauge what step on the list that you think the youth may be on. It would be beneficial to use this tool in conjunction with the strategies described in the Pathway to Hope section of this book.

1. **God's love.** I am beginning to understand how much God loves me and that God's love is my anchor.
2. **Realization.** I know my life has much value because God created me for a purpose.
3. **Belief.** I am capable, confident, and optimistic, and I have hope (aspirations) for my future.
4. **Action.** I establish goals and paths to achieve my goals because I know I have a future.
5. **God's truth.** I trust in God and believe in His Word. His Word is my truth.

CHAPTER 5

Hope for the Caregiver

Caregivers can often become weary as a result of vicarious trauma, also known as compassion fatigue, or an overwhelming caseload. Numerous other responsibilities can result in fatigue, emotional exhaustion, burnout, feeling overwhelmed, or a feeling that your emotional gas tank is getting low or empty. Caregiving can even result in a negative mindset or loss of hope in your own life. But that is not God's will for your life. Your self-care is of utmost importance. You must rest, recharge and renew. God wants you whole—spirit, soul, mind, and body. First Thessalonians 5:23 NIV says, "Now may God Himself, the God of peace, sanctify you through and through. May your whole spirit, soul and body be kept blameless at the coming of our Lord."

You must be intentional about making self-care a priority in order to mitigate or avoid burnout. Here a few tips for self-care recommended by the organization Mental Health First Aid USA:

Take a deep breath and step away.
Protect your time and space.
Establish healthy boundaries.
Be kind to yourself.
Ask for help.
Write it out.

In addition to these practical steps, spiritual nourishment is of utmost importance. Matthew 11:28-29 NIV says,

> "Come to Me all who are weary and burdened and I will give you rest. Take my yoke upon you and learn from Me, for I am gentle and humble in heart and you will find rest for your souls."

It is also important to be mindful that God will do the heavy lifting, to check your fuel tank and to learn to recognize the signs that your tank is nearing empty. Signs may include a loss of satisfaction, joy, or motivation. Sometimes you may even feel unqualified for the task. During these times, it is important for you to go back to your source—the source that brings you peace and strength. For me, that source of peace and strength is my Heavenly Father. When I feel my fuel tank getting low, I cry out to my Papa, my Heavenly Father, and I pour out my heart to Him. Then I ask Him to restore my joy so that I rest in His presence. "He restores my soul" (Psalm 23:3).

One final tip is to remember to love yourself. Your life has value, your life has significance, your life has great worth.

The Importance of Being Soul-Aware

My son, Pastor Touré Roberts, released his third book last year, titled *Balance: Positioning Yourself to Do All Things Well*. In *Balance*, he talks about being not just self-aware but also soul-aware. Here is what he concludes about being soul-aware:

> Balance requires listening to your soul, not to the noise around you. The person who will find Balance must learn the discipline of regularly muting life's noise. Learning effective ways of stillness allows us to tap into the rhythm of the soul, which leads right into Balance.

CHAPTER 6

Closing Thoughts

Please know that you matter and that God sees you. You have a special place in His heart as a caregiver of children and youth because children are so important to Him. He is cheering for you as you invest in the lives of young people. God is all-powerful and He will do the heavy lifting as you sow seeds of hope that can impact generations to come. One person who has hope can play a part in breaking generational cycles of hopelessness and despair in a family. I believe that you will reap blessings of joy and satisfaction knowing that you had a part in transforming a young person's life from hopelessness to hope. What a privilege and an honor!

I pray that this book will be a source of encouragement and support as you go about your day. May it be a reminder that you play a pivotal role in the young lives entrusted to you. I pray that you will use it as an instruction manual or toolkit to help instill hope or renew hope in the children and youth who are under your authority or sphere of influence. That you will be strengthened and confident that better days are ahead for them as well as yourself. I pray that your hope will be renewed, that you will know you are qualified for the task, and that you will know God sees you, loves you, and is cheering for you.

Because I know that praying the Word brings results, and if we ask anything according to His will, we can have confidence that He hears us (First John 5:14) I close with this prayer for you.

Dear Heavenly Father,

I ask You, the God of hope, to fill each caregiver with all joy and peace in believing that they may abound in hope, through the power of the Holy Ghost.[Romans 15:13]

I ask that You give every caregiver reading this book strength and tenacity to remain committed and faithful in this important and urgent task. Open their spiritual eyes to understand the warfare youth in their sphere of influence face, and give each caregiver wisdom and confidence in their ability to instill or restore hope in those youth. May they not grow weary in well-doing, and I thank You that they shall reap if they faint not.[Galatian 6:9]

I pray that each caregiver grows in their knowledge of You, and that if they haven't already done so, they will enter into a relationship with Your Son Jesus Christ, our Savior; that each caregiver will know the depth of Your love for them;[Ephesians 3:18] that they will experience your power; and that they too will have renewed hope for the future.

In Jesus's name, amen.

I close with the words of Mother Teresa: "In Hope we rely utterly on the omnipotence of Him who said, "without Me you can do nothing.'"

APPENDIX

Scriptures to Renew
or Inspire Hope

Those that hope in the Lord shall renew their strength. (Isaiah 40:31a)

Why are you downcast within, O my soul?
And why are you disquieted within me?
Hope in God, for I shall yet praise Him
for the help of His countenance . (Psalm 42:5)

For whatsoever things were written aforetime were written for our learning, that we through patience and comfort of the Scriptures might have hope. (Romans 15:4)

The Lord is my portion, saith my soul. Therefore will I hope in Him. (Lamentations 3:24)

Be of good courage,
And He shall strengthen your heart,
All who hope in the Lord. (Psalm 31:24)

Christ in me. The hope of glory. (Colossians 1:27b)

I am the Lord. Those that hope in me shall not be disappointed. (Isaiah 49:23b NIV)

Behold, the eye of the Lord is on those who fear Him,
On those who hope in His mercy. (Psalm 33:18)

I wait for the Lord, my soul waits,
And in His Word I do hope. (Psalm 130:5)

Thou art my hiding place and my shield.
I hope in Your word. (Psalm 119:114)

Let us hold fast to our profession of faith without wavering; for He is faithful that promised.
(Hebrews 10:23)

Wait on the Lord,
Be of good courage,
And He shall strengthen your heart;
Wait I say on the Lord. (Psalm 27:14)

FURTHER READING

Cheering for the Children, Casey Gwinn

Hope Rising, Casey Gwinn, JD, and Chan Hellman, PhD

Break Every Chain, John Eckhardt

Psychology of Hope, C. R. Snyder

Balance, Touré Roberts

SAMPLE WORKSHEETS

_____: All About Me

your name

I am interested in

I am good at

My strengths are

I am proud of myself because

Something I would like to improve in is

An immediate goal that I have for myself is

What I like about me is

Challenges or obstacles I face are

I can overcome these obstacles by

Fears I sometimes have are

My dream or vision (my aspiration) for my future is

Something super special or unique about me is

> "The only person you are destined to become is the person you decide to be"
>
> Ralph Waldo Emerson

WISE
GOALS

MY MAIN GOAL RIGHT NOW

MY NO.1 GOAL IS... ....
....

TARGET DATE

How will I know I've reached my goal?
....
....

My key strengths that will help me achieve this goal are...
1. ....
2. ....
3. ....
4. ....
5. ....

This goal is important to me because...
....
....
....
....
....

Obstacles that may arise are...
1. ....
2. ....
3. ....
4. ....
5. ....

How I plan to respond to each obstacle:
→ ....
→ ....
→ ....
→ ....
→ ....

What will be different when I achieve my goal?
....
....
....
....
....

NEXT BEST STEPS
1. .... ☐
2. .... ☐
3. .... ☐
4. .... ☐
5. .... ☐

© wisegoals.com

Printed in the United States
by Baker & Taylor Publisher Services